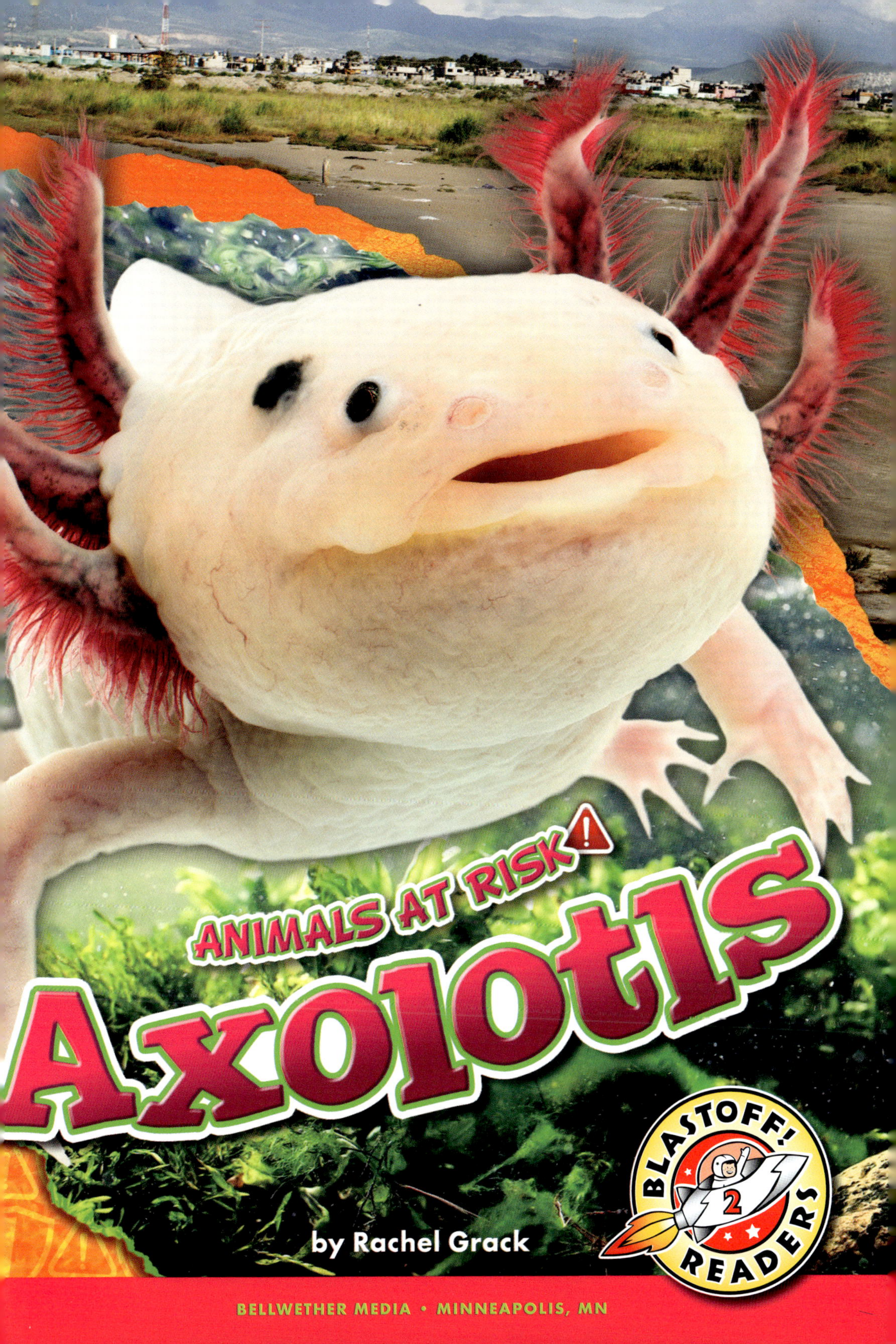

ANIMALS AT RISK

Axolotls

by Rachel Grack

BELLWETHER MEDIA • MINNEAPOLIS, MN

Blastoff! Readers are carefully developed by literacy experts to build reading stamina and move students toward fluency by combining standards-based content with developmentally appropriate text.

Level 1 provides the most support through repetition of high-frequency words, light text, predictable sentence patterns, and strong visual support.

Level 2 offers early readers a bit more challenge through varied sentences, increased text load, and text-supportive special features.

Level 3 advances early-fluent readers toward fluency through increased text load, less reliance on photos, advancing concepts, longer sentences, and more complex special features.

★ **Blastoff! Universe**

Reading Level

Grade K

Grades 1–3

Grade 4

This edition first published in 2023 by Bellwether Media, Inc.

Library of Congress Cataloging-in-Publication Data

Names: Koestler-Grack, Rachel A., 1973- author.
Title: Axolotls / by Rachel Grack.
Description: Minneapolis, MN : Bellwether Media, Inc., 2023. | Series: Blastoff! Readers. Animals at Risk | Includes bibliographical references and index. | Audience: Ages 5-8 | Audience: Grades 2-3 | Summary: "Relevant images match informative text in this introduction to axolotls. Intended for students in kindergarten through third grade"-- Provided by publisher.
Identifiers: LCCN 2022037567 (print) | LCCN 2022037568 (ebook) | ISBN 9798886871180 (library binding) | ISBN 9798886872446 (ebook)
Subjects: LCSH: Axolotls--Juvenile literature.
Classification: LCC QL668.C23 K64 2023 (print) | LCC QL668.C23 (ebook) | DDC 597.8/58--dc23/eng/20220811
LC record available at https://lccn.loc.gov/2022037567
LC ebook record available at https://lccn.loc.gov/2022037568

Editor: Kieran Downs Designer: Brittany McIntosh

Printed in the United States of America, North Mankato, MN.

Table of Contents

Smiling Swimmers

Axolotls are strange **amphibians**. They have feathery **gills** and long tails.

They swim like fish.
But they have legs.
Their faces seem to smile.

Axolotls only live in one lake.
It is in Mexico City, Mexico.
Some swim in nearby **canals**, too.

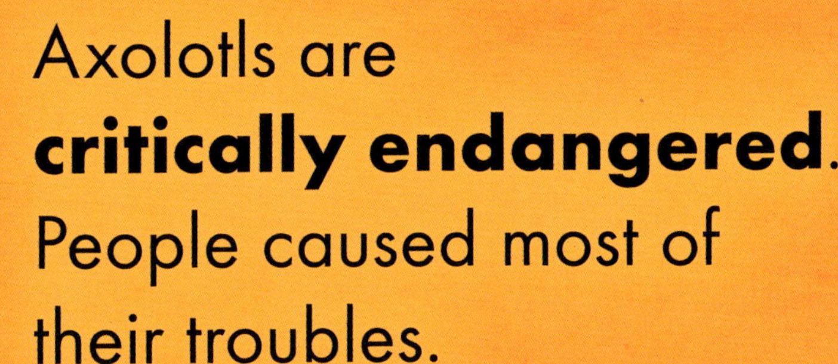

Axolotls are **critically endangered**. People caused most of their troubles.

Axolotl Range

N

W E

S

range =

In Danger!

axolotl habitat

Axolotls' **habitat** is getting smaller. People **drained** the lake they live in. This kept it from flooding.

People also build near the lake. **Pollution** has made the water dirty.

people build near the lake

water becomes dirty

axolotls lose habitat

Axolotls were once at the top of the **food chain**. But people added new fish to the lake.

These fish eat axolotl eggs and young.

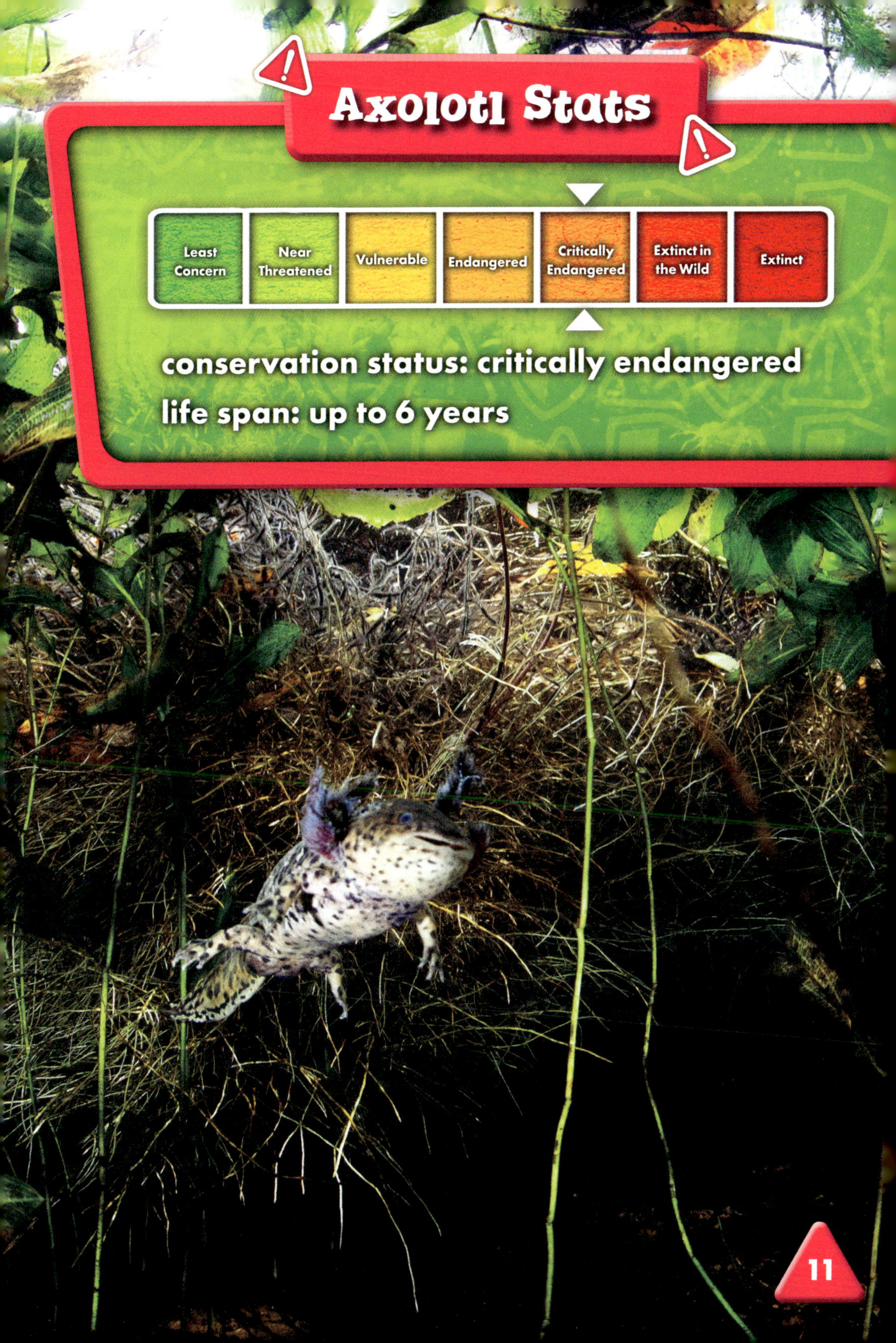
Axolotl Stats
Least Concern
Near Threatened
Vulnerable
Endangered
Critically Endangered
Extinct in the Wild
Extinct
conservation status: critically endangered
life span: up to 6 years

Save the Axolotls!

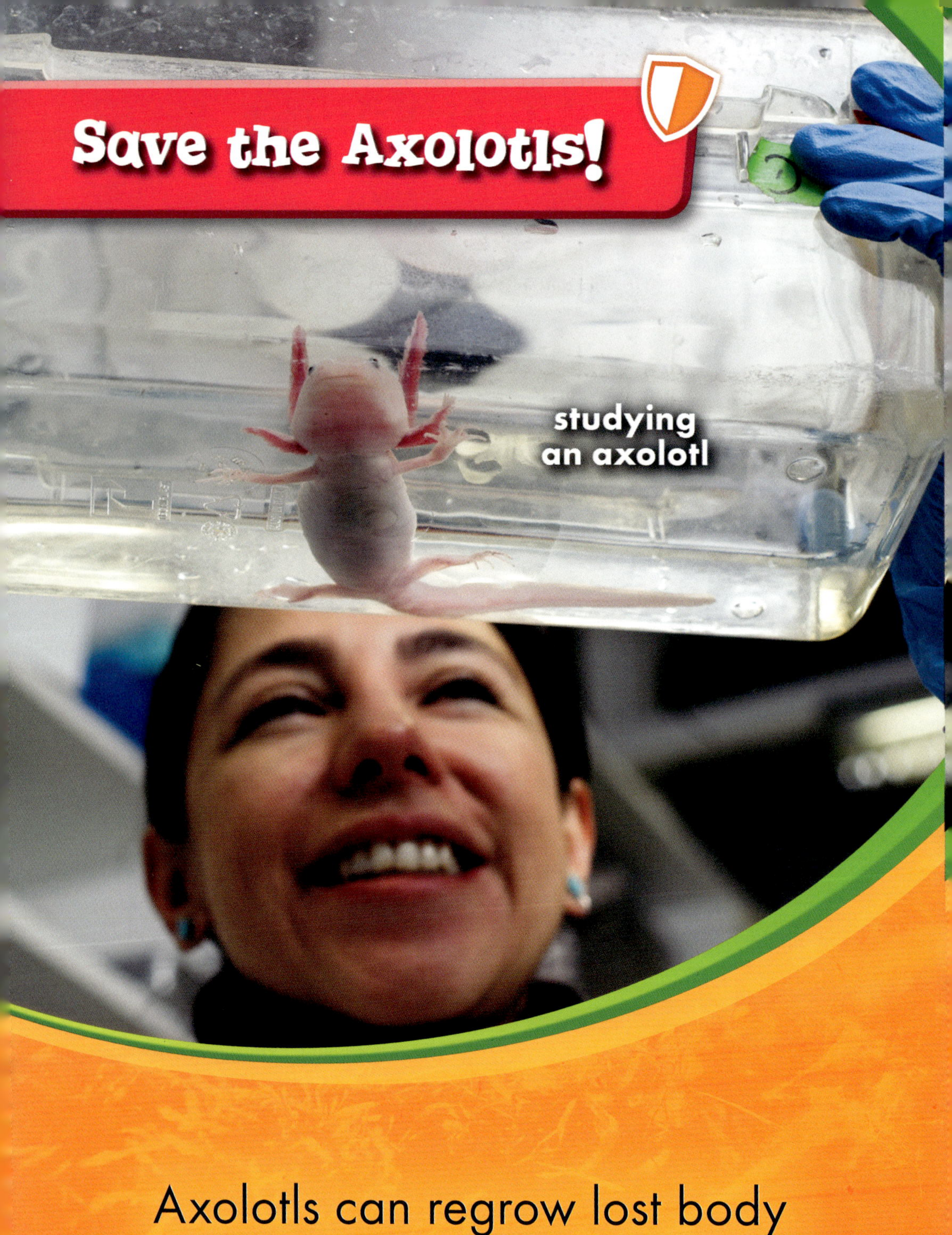

studying an axolotl

Axolotls can regrow lost body parts. This could help people.

Doctors want the chance to study them more. They might learn new ways to **treat** sicknesses.

The World with Axolotls

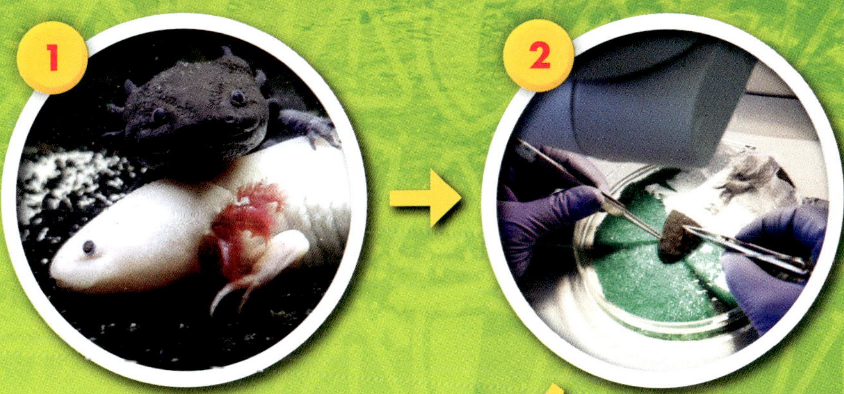

more wild axolotls

doctors can study them

new ways to help people

Axolotls need healthy homes. Farmers make floating gardens.

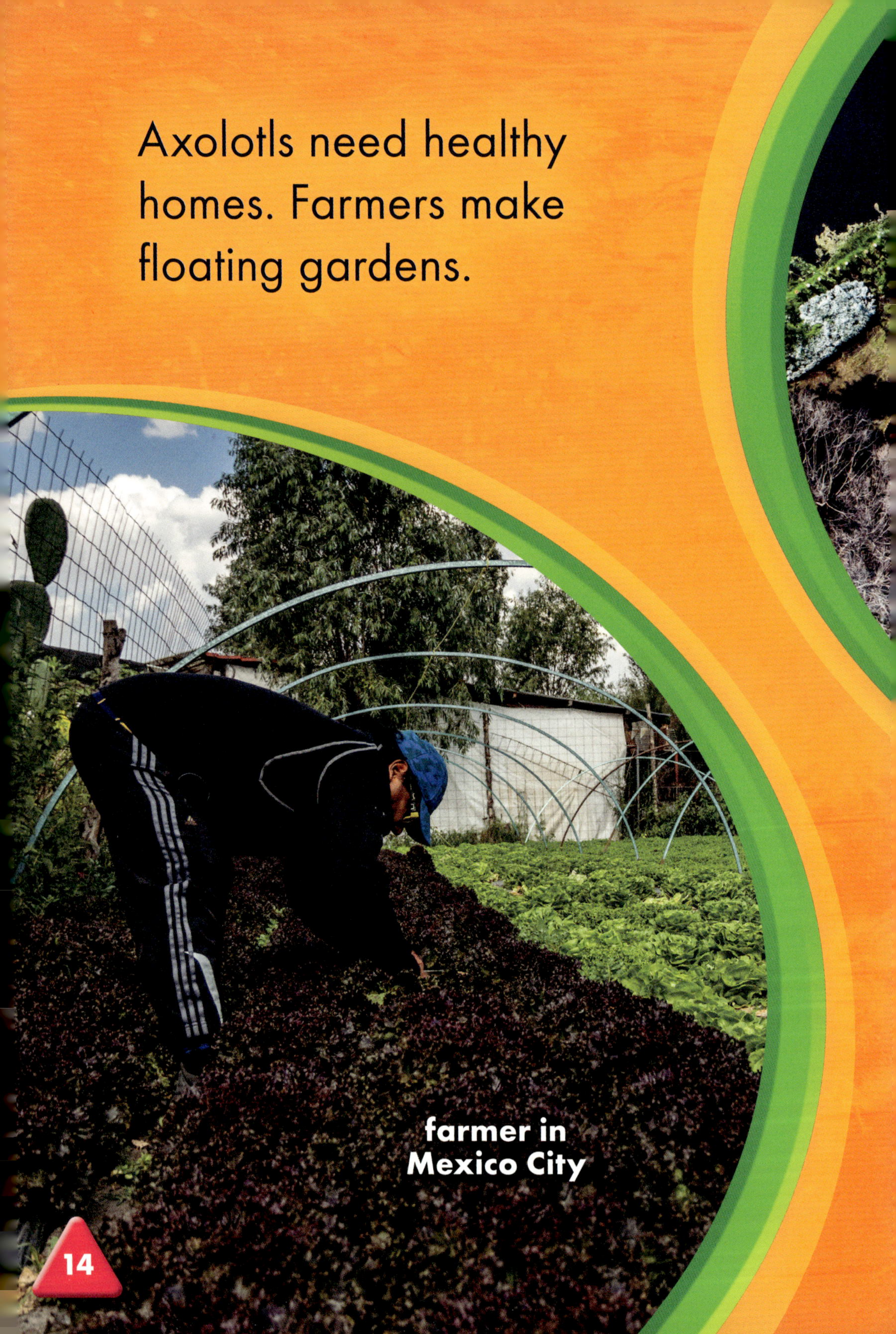

farmer in Mexico City

These gardens are made of plants and mud. They **filter** the water. The water stays clean.

fisherman sweeping a lake

Fishermen keep axolotls safe from **predators**. They **sweep** the lake.

This removes harmful fish. Fewer axolotl eggs and young are eaten.

People can learn about axolotls. They may want to help save them.

visiting the lake

People can travel to visit the lake.
They can teach others to help.

Donations help wildlife groups save axolotls. Buying food from earth-friendly farms also helps.

Everyone can work to keep axolotls smiling!

Glossary

amphibians—cold-blooded animals that live in water and breathe with gills when young; axolotls keep their gills for life.

canals—waterways that connect to a lake

critically endangered—greatly in danger of dying out

donations—gifts, usually money

drained—removed water

filter—to make cleaner

food chain—a system of who eats what in a habitat

gills—parts along the side of an animal that help it breathe underwater

habitat—a place where animals live

pollution—substances that make nature dirty; pollution usually comes from humans.

predators—animals that hunt other animals for food

sweep—to catch as many fish as possible in a certain place

treat—to care for a person or an animal with a sickness

To Learn More

AT THE LIBRARY

Bassier, Emily. *Axolotls.* Minneapolis, Minn.: Pop!, 2020.

Jaycox, Jaclyn. *Axolotls.* North Mankato, Minn.: Pebble, 2023.

Grack, Rachel. *Sea Turtles.* Minneapolis, Minn.: Bellwether Media, 2022.

ON THE WEB

FACTSURFER

Factsurfer.com gives you a safe, fun way to find more information.

1. Go to www.factsurfer.com.

2. Enter "axolotls" into the search box and click 🔍.

3. Select your book cover to see a list of related content.

Index

The images in this book are reproduced through the courtesy of: Life on white/ Alamy Stock Photo, front cover; Eric Isselee, p. 3; Spok 83, pp. 4, 18; Lapis2380, p. 5; mike lane/ Alamy Stock Photo, p. 6; Jon Lovette/ Alamy Stock Photo, p. 8; LukeandKarla.Travel, p. 9 (top left); Octavio Hoyos, p. 9 (top right); PRILL, p. 9 (bottom); blickwinkel/ Alamy Stock Photo, p. 10; Alejandro Prieto/ Nature Picture Library, pp. 10-11; ROBERT MICHAEL/ Stringer/ Getty Images, p. 12; Ground Picture, p. 13 (bottom); Leoncio Jesus Ruiz de la Garza/ Alamy Stock Photo, p. 14; Francisco Gomez Sosa, p. 15; AFP Contributor/ Contributor/ Getty Images, pp. 16, 17; marketa1982, p. 19; aureapterus/ Getty Images, p. 20; Cherokee4/ Alamy Stock Photo, pp. 20-21; IrinaK, p. 23.